CW01510845

TAVIL...

Travel Guide 2025

A Guide Through History, Culture and
Must-see Attractions of Portugal's Timeless
Seaside Gem.

Edna G. Reeves

©[2025] [Edna G. Reeves]

All rights reserved.
No part of this book may be reproduced, stored in a retrieval system, or transmitted in any form or by any means—electronic, mechanical, photocopying, recording, or otherwise—without the prior written permission of the publisher, except in the case of brief quotations embodied in reviews and certain other noncommercial uses permitted by copyright law.

Disclaimer
This travel guide is based on research and information available at the time of publication. While every effort has been made to ensure accuracy, the publisher and authors assume no responsibility for any errors, omissions, or changes that may occur. Readers are advised to verify details such as visa requirements, transportation schedules, business hours, and safety guidelines before traveling. The inclusion of any business, service, or recommendation does not imply endorsement. Travelers are responsible for their own decisions and actions.

Table of Content

Introduction to Tavira.

Tavira, located along the sun-kissed coastline of Portugal's Algarve area, is a hidden gem that seamlessly combines old-world elegance with a carefree beach attitude. Tavira, unlike the bustling tourist hubs of the Algarve, remains delightfully real, with cobbled alleys and whitewashed cottages covered with classic azulejo tiles. The calm flow of the Gilão River adds to its obvious allure.

Tavira, known as one of Portugal's most gorgeous cities, is a place where time pauses, enabling visitors to immerse themselves in its rich history, vibrant culture, and spectacular natural beauty. Tavira provides a wonderful getaway from the everyday, whether you're strolling through its ancient center, indulging in fresh seafood at a riverfront café, or simply soaking up the sun on one of its pristine beaches.

Beyond its postcard-perfect surroundings, what truly distinguishes Tavira is its atmosphere—charming yet unassuming, serene yet vibrant. It's a location where local fisherman still go out for their daily catch, where traditional festivals liven up the streets, and where every corner holds a story waiting to be told.

Historical Background.

Tavira's history is as interesting as its scenery, dating back over 3,000 years. Its history dates back to the 8th century BCE, when the Phoenicians settled here, enticed by the region's strategic location and plentiful natural resources. The town later thrived under the Romans, who built bridges, roads, and aqueducts, some of which still exist today and provide an intriguing peek into Tavira's historic past.

With the fall of the Roman Empire, Tavira saw periods of decline and transformation before falling under Moorish dominion in the eighth century CE. The Moors altered the town by bringing advanced irrigation systems, architectural influences, and cultural traditions that still determine Tavira's identity. The relics of their presence may still be seen in the town's complex rooftops, whitewashed buildings, and the remains of the medieval castle, which formerly served as a fortification against invaders.

Tavira was recaptured by Christian armies in 1242 as part of the Portuguese Reconquista, led by King Dom Paio Peres Correia. The town experienced a golden age in the 16th and 17th centuries, becoming one of the Algarve's most important trading ports. It was a hub for fishing, salt manufacture, and commerce, with ships moving between Portugal and the remote reaches of the world. However, Tavira's wealth was shattered in 1755 by a terrible earthquake, which changed the geography and reduced the city's marine significance.

Despite historical struggles, Tavira has remained robust, retaining its architectural splendor, cultural richness, and timeless charm. Today, it serves as a living museum, with centuries of history woven into its streets, churches, and traditions, providing tourists with a profound and meaningful link to Portugal's past.

Geographical Setting

Tavira is located in the eastern Algarve, approximately 30 kilometers east of Faro and near the Spanish border. Unlike the towering cliffs and rough coastlines of other sections of the Algarve, this region has a more pleasant landscape, with rolling hills, beautiful salt marshes, and broad sandy beaches. Tavira is situated on the banks of the Gilão River, which flows through the town and eventually joins the Atlantic Ocean.

Tavira's topography is defined by its closeness to the Ria Formosa Natural Park, a magnificent lagoon system that runs down the Algarve coast. This protected region is home to a variety of animals, including migrating birds, flamingos, and uncommon species, making it a haven for nature enthusiasts and birdwatchers. The park's tranquil rivers, sandbanks, and barrier islands provide a stunning backdrop for outdoor activities ranging from kayaking and boat tours to beautiful hikes across salt flats and coastal dunes.

Tavira's shoreline includes some of Portugal's most stunning and untouched beaches. The most well-known is llha de Tavira, a golden-sand island accessible only by boat that boasts crystal-clear waters, laidback beach bars, and a true escape into nature. Other adjacent beaches, including Praia do Barril and

Cabanas Beach, offer equally beautiful settings for sunbathing, swimming, and exploration.

Tavira is surrounded by picturesque countryside towns, orchards of almond and fig trees, and the Serra do Caldeirão hills, which offer a stunning contrast to the town's coastal environment. Whether you're drawn to Tavira's historic alleys, the peacefulness of its beaches, or the undisturbed beauty of the natural park, this lovely town has a geographical diversity that will appeal to any type of traveler.

Tavira, with its rich history, breathtaking landscapes, and inviting environment, is a destination that captures hearts and stays in minds long after the journey is over. Whether you're here for the first time or returning to rediscover its allure, this town offers a blend of timeless beauty, cultural richness, and seaside peace.

Planning Your Trip to Tavira.

Tavira is a must-see destination in Portugal's Algarve area, seamlessly combining history, culture, and natural beauty. Whether you're planning a short trip or a longer stay, knowing when to go, how to get there, and how to travel around will help you have a relaxing and enjoyable vacation.

Best time to visit

Tavira's Mediterranean climate makes it a year-round destination, although the best time to visit is based on your tastes.

Spring (March-May): Ideal for sightseeing and nature lovers.

Spring is one of the greatest times to visit Tavira because the temperatures are pleasant (15°C to 25°C) and the town is less busy. The landscape comes alive with flowering wildflowers, giving it an ideal time to visit the Ria Formosa Natural Park and enjoy outdoor activities such as hiking and cycling. Easter events give a cultural component to your vacation.

Summer (June-August) - Ideal for Beachgoers

Summer is the best season to go to the beach and enjoy the sun. Tavira's beaches, such as Ilha de Tavira and Praia do Barril, are at their peak, with temperatures ranging from 25°C to 35°C and long, sunny days. However, this is also the busiest season, resulting in increased lodging costs and more tourists. It is advised that you book in advance.

Autumn (September-November) - Ideal for a Relaxed Experience

Early autumn is an excellent time to visit Tavira. The weather stays mild (20°C to 30°C in September, gradually cooling by November), summer crowds have dissipated, and the sea is still suitable for swimming. It's also harvest season, so you can eat fresh local vegetables and attend cultural events like the Festival of St. Martin in November.

Winter (December-February): Quiet and Authentic

Winter in Tavira is pleasant, with temperatures rarely falling below 10°C. While it's too cold to swim, it's an ideal time to visit the town's historic buildings without crowds. Many restaurants and sights remain open, allowing you to enjoy Tavira as the locals do.

Recommendation: Visit Tavira in May, September, or October for a balanced experience with nice weather, fewer crowds, and affordable costs.

Getting To Tavira

Tavira is well-connected to major Portuguese cities and adjacent Spain, making it easily accessible by aircraft, rail, bus, or vehicle.

By Air: Flying into Faro Airport

Tavira's nearest airport is Faro Airport (FAO), which is approximately 40 kilometers west of the town. Faro Airport handles a large number of international flights, primarily from Europe, with regular connections to Lisbon, Porto, and major UK cities.

How to Get From Faro Airport to Tavira:
- **Train:** Take a taxi or bus from the airport to Faro Train Station, then catch a train to Tavira (40-50 minutes).
- **Bus:** The journey from Faro Airport to Faro city center takes around 15 minutes. From Faro Bus Station, take a

Rede Expressos or local EVA Transportes bus to Tavira (1 hour).

- **Taxi/Rideshare:** A direct taxi or Uber from Faro Airport to Tavira takes about 30-40 minutes and costs between €40 and €50.
- **Car Rental:** Renting a car is an excellent alternative if you want to explore beyond Tavira. The A22 highway connects Faro to Tavira in around 30 minutes.

By Train: A scenic journey.

Portugal's rail network provides an easy way to get to Tavira. The Algarve Line connects Lagos to Vila Real de Santo António, stopping in Tavira along the way. If traveling from Lisbon or Porto, board a long-distance train to Faro and then transfer to the Algarve Line for the final portion of the journey.

- **Lisbon to Tavira**: about. 4.5 hours (from Lisbon Oriente Station to Faro, then transfer to a local train).
- **Faro to Tavira:** about. 40-50 minutes (€3 to €5).

Bus: Cost-effective Option

Long-distance buses connect Tavira to other Portuguese cities. The Rede Expressos and FlixBus networks provide direct routes from Lisbon, Porto, and other Algarve towns.

- **Lisbon to Tavira**: about. 4.5 hours (€20-25).
- **Faro to Tavira:** about. 1 hour (€5-€7).

Buses are a cheaper option to trains, but they take somewhat longer because of stops along the way.

By Car: Flexibility for Exploration

Driving to Tavira is an excellent option if you want to explore the Algarve's beach and countryside areas at your leisure. The A22 motorway (toll road) connects Tavira to Faro, Lisbon, and Spain, while the N125 road provides a more scenic but slower alternative.

- **Faro to Tavira** takes 30-40 minutes via the A22.
- **Lisbon to Tavira** takes 2.5 to 3 hours via the A2 and A22.

Tavira is a convenient cross-border destination, as it is only two hours from Seville (Spain).

Transportation in Tavira

Tavira's tiny size and excellent local transportation options make traveling about easy once you arrive.

Walking - The best way to explore the town.

Tavira's historic core is easily walkable, with nearby attractions, attractive streets, and the gorgeous Gilão River. Some streets are cobblestoned and slightly hilly, so wear comfortable shoes.

Public Buses - Cost-effective for Short Distances

Tavira has a minor urban bus network operated by EVA Transportes that serves essential regions including as the bus and train stations, shopping districts, and certain residential neighborhoods. While buses are uncommon, they are useful for traveling to surrounding towns such as Cabanas and Santa Luzia.

Taxis and Rideshares: Convenient for Short Journeys

Taxis are accessible in Tavira, with ranks at Praça da República and the bus station. Uber and Bolt also operate in the neighborhood, typically offering less expensive and more convenient options. A normal cab ride within town costs between €5 and €10.

Car Rental - Ideal for Exploring Nearby Areas

Renting a car is not required for traveling around Tavira, although it is recommended if you intend to visit surrounding beaches, countryside villages, or other Algarve destinations. Parking in the town center may be limited, so check for free parking areas around the Gran Plaza Shopping Center or the Gilão River.

Bicycles and Scooters: A Fun Alternative.

Tavira is relatively flat, so cycling is a fun way to get around. Several rental shops provide bicycles and e-scooters for touring the town or cycling to Praia do Barril along the picturesque Ecovia do Algarve cycling path.

Boat Services: Essential for Island Beaches

To reach Ilha de Tavira, take the ferry from Tavira Quay or Quatro Águas. In the summer, boats run regularly (every 15-30 minutes), however in the winter, timetables are more limited.

With a little planning, your trip to Tavira will be stress-free. Whether you arrive by plane, rail, or automobile, and whether you choose to walk or rent a bike, seeing this charming town is simple and pleasurable.

Accommodation options in Tavira

Tavira has a wide selection of lodging options to accommodate all travelers, from opulent hotels with breathtaking views to quaint boutique guesthouses and low-cost stays. Tavira has something for everyone, whether you're searching for a romantic break, a family-friendly hideaway, or a small spot to enjoy true local friendliness.

Luxury Hotels Offer Comfort and Elegance

Tavira offers a variety of luxury hotels with top-tier amenities, outstanding service, and breathtaking surroundings for guests seeking a high-end experience. Many are located in historical structures, providing a unique blend of modern comfort and traditional charm.

What to Expect at Luxury Hotels:
- Spacious, nicely appointed rooms
- High-end amenities include pools, spas, and fine dining restaurants
- Prime settings, frequently near rivers or historical landmarks.

- Personalized service and attention to detail.

Top luxury hotels in Tavira:
Pousada Convento de Tavira - Housed in a beautifully renovated 16th-century convent, this boutique luxury hotel provides a tranquil environment with elegant rooms, a swimming pool, and a fine-dining restaurant. Ideal for those who value history and peace.

AP Cabanas Beach & Nature - A trendy, eco-friendly resort near Ria Formosa Natural Park that offers modern rooms, a spa, and direct boat access to Cabanas Beach. Perfect for couples and nature enthusiasts.

Vila Galé Tavira - A large, premium hotel with a Moorish-inspired style that has a spacious pool, a wellness center, and an excellent position near the historic center. An excellent alternative for families and leisure tourists.

Who Should Stay at a Luxury Hotel?
- Couples seeking a romantic getaway.
- Travelers who prefer superior amenities and comfort

- Visitors who enjoy historical and beautiful areas

Boutique Guest Houses: Authentic and Cozy.

Boutique guesthouses offer a more intimate and locally inspired experience. These hotels are frequently run by locals, resulting in a personalized experience with distinct character and charm.

What to Expect at Boutique Guest houses:
- Rooms are thoughtfully created with a blend of modern and classic decor.
- Hosts provide warm, personal service and might give insider travel suggestions.
- Homey atmosphere, particularly in renovated townhouses or converted buildings.
- Breakfast usually includes local specialties.

Top Boutique Guest Houses in Tavira:
The São Paulo Boutique Hotel: housed in a beautifully restored home, features modern rooms, a serene courtyard, and an appealing

pool. It's an excellent combination of comfort and local character.

Tavira House: a small historic residence with individually decorated rooms, a picturesque rooftop patio, and a warm atmosphere.

Casa Beleza do Sul: is a beautifully built guesthouse that seems like a home away from home, with artistic furnishings and a convenient location near Tavira's main attractions.

Who should stay at a boutique guesthouse?

- Couples and solitary travelers seeking a charming and distinctive stay.
- Individuals who value personalized service and local recommendations
- Visitors who enjoy a blend of history, comfort, and authenticity.

Budget-Friendly Accommodations: Comfortable and affordable

If you're traveling on a budget, Tavira has plenty of inexpensive lodgings that offer great value without sacrificing comfort. Budget hotels, hostels, and basic guesthouses make it possible to experience Tavira without going overboard.

What to Expect from Budget-Friendly Stays:
- Clean, basic rooms with necessary amenities.
- Friendly and inviting environment
- Convenient placement near public transportation and major attractions.
- Bathrooms are either shared or private, depending on the property.

Best Budget-Friendly Accommodations in Tavira

Hi Tavira Pousada de Juventude - This youth hostel is an excellent choice for backpackers and budget visitors, offering dormitory-style rooms and private alternatives at reasonable prices.

Residencial Mares - A simple yet pleasant guesthouse with a great riverbank location that offers affordable accommodations with a touch of traditional charm.

Lagoas - A modest, family-run hotel providing affordable rooms and convenient access to Tavira's town center and beach.

Who Should Stay at a Budget-Friendly Accommodation?

- Backpackers and single travelers seeking low-cost accommodations
- Families or groups looking for an affordable stay
- Visitors that intend to spend the majority of their time exploring rather than in their accommodation.

Vacation Rentals: Flexibility and Home Comforts.

Vacation homes are a great alternative to hotels if you want more space, privacy, or the convenience of self-catering. Tavira offers a choice of apartments, villas, and holiday houses that are ideal for extended visits or group travel.

What to Expect From Vacation Rentals:
- Fully equipped kitchens for self-catering.
- More space, including living areas and perhaps private terraces or gardens.
- A local, residential atmosphere, often in picturesque surroundings.

- Excellent choices for families, digital nomads, and long-term guests.

Top Areas for Vacation Rentals:
- **Historic Center** - Stay in a classic townhouse near Tavira's main attractions, perfect for those who enjoy walking.
- **Cabanas de Tavira** - An excellent location for seaside flats and villas, ideal for families and beachgoers.
- **Santa Luzia** - known as the "Octopus Capital," is a tranquil fishing community with beautiful waterfront vistas and a local feel.
- **Pedras d'el Rei** - A resort-style enclave near Praia do Barril that offers a mix of flats and villas with easy beach access.

Who Should Stay in a Vacation Rental?
- Families or groups that require additional room and culinary amenities.
- Travelers planning a longer stay in Tavira.
- Visitors seeking a more independent and homelike experience.

Final Thoughts: Selecting the Right Accommodation

When choose where to stay in Tavira, consider your travel style, budget, and desired degree of comfort.

If you want luxury and full-service amenities, choose a high-end hotel such as Pousada Convento de Tavira.

A boutique guesthouse, such as São Paulo Boutique Hotel, provides a lovely and private experience.

If you're traveling on a budget, hostels or low-cost guesthouses like Residencial Mares are excellent options.

If you require more space and flexibility, a vacation property in Cabanas de Tavira or Santa Luzia may be the ideal solution.

Regardless of where you stay, Tavira's pleasant environment, stunning surroundings, and rich history will make your visit memorable.

Must-see Attractions in Tavira

Tavira is a town where history whispers through cobblestone lanes, the river rushes past centuries-old houses, and every turn exposes a piece of Portugal's history. When visiting this delightful Algarve jewel, you must see three landmarks: Tavira Castle, the Roman Bridge (Ponte Romana), and the Igreja do Misericórdia. Each of these locations provides a unique story, ranging from medieval warfare to historic trade networks and religious art. So, let's go back in time and find out why these sites should be on your Tavira bucket list.

Tavira Castle: A Window into the Past.

Tavira Castle (Castelo de Tavira) sits on a small hill overlooking the town, silently guarding centuries of history. While its towering stone walls may not be as fearsome as they once were, the castle is nevertheless a beautiful sight, providing a glimpse into Tavira's medieval past as well as some of the best panoramic views in town.

A Castle Born of Conflict

The castle's beginnings can be traced back to Moorish dominance in the eighth century, when Islamic rulers of the Iberian Peninsula constructed a fortress to protect their settlement. For nearly 400 years, the castle protected Tavira from invaders, staying strong as the town grew under Moorish influence. However, in 1242, during Portugal's Christian Reconquista, King Dom Paio Peres Correia led an attack to retake Tavira. According to legend, Christian armies broke through the castle walls with the help of nuns from a nearby monastery, who smuggled them inside.

Following their conquest, the Portuguese expanded the castle, strengthening its walls and watchtowers. It remained an important military construction for generations, but the 1755 Lisbon earthquake badly devastated it, leaving just the ruins we see today.

Exploring the Castle Today

Walking within the castle gates, one can practically hear the echoes of past wars. Inside, the open space has been transformed into a stunning Mediterranean garden, with brilliant flowers and lush greenery growing against the backdrop of aged stone walls.

What's the true highlight? Climbing the ancient ramparts. As you climb the narrow steps to the top of the castle walls, you will be rewarded with breathtaking 360-degree views of Tavira. Views include the town's terracotta rooftops, the Gilão River, and the Atlantic Ocean in the distance. It's the ideal location for admiring Tavira's natural beauty and taking wonderful images.

Roman Bridge (Ponte Romana): A Timeless Crossing.

The Roman Bridge (Ponte Romana), a lovely stone bridge that gracefully arches over the Gilão River, is one of Tavira's most picturesque locations. Though it's sometimes referred to as a "Roman" bridge, the current structure dates back to the 17th century, and was built on prior foundations that may have had Roman origins. Regardless of its precise age, the bridge remains one of Tavira's most recognizable emblems.

A Bridge with Many Stories

The original bridge most likely dates back to Roman times, when Tavira was a major trading hub along the Algarve coast. To travel between

Lisbon and southern Spain, Roman merchants and soldiers required a reliable crossing over the Gilão River. Over the ages, the bridge was repaired and improved, eventually becoming the stone structure we see today.

For decades, the Ponte Romana served as Tavira's lifeline, linking the town's two sides. Fishermen, traders, and travelers crossed on a daily basis, and throughout the Middle Ages, it was a critical route for soldiers protecting Tavira from assault. It was closed to car traffic in 1989, making it a pedestrian-only path that would preserve its splendor for future generations.

Walking Across History
Today, wandering across the seven-arched bridge is one of Tavira's most delightful activities. The view from the bridge's center is breathtaking: on one side, colorful residences and cafés line the riverbank, while on the other, little boats bob softly in the water, representing Tavira's placid rhythm of life.

At sunset, the bridge becomes even more spectacular, as the sky becomes orange and pink and the medieval town glows in the mellow evening sunlight. Locals and travelers alike come here to appreciate the scenery, making it an ideal location for a romantic evening stroll or a quiet moment of introspection.

Igreja da Misericórdia

Among Tavira's numerous churches, Igreja do Misericórdia stands out as a magnificent architectural masterpiece. Built in the 16th century, this Renaissance and Baroque-style church is regarded as one of the best specimens of ecclesiastical art in the Algarve.

A Church Built With Devotion

The Misericórdia Brotherhood, a religious charity dedicated to helping the impoverished and sick, commissioned the church. Construction began in 1541, during Portugal's Age of Discovery, a period when the country's wealth from overseas colonies enabled the construction of large religious structures.

One of the church's most notable features is its ornate façade, which is regarded as one of the most beautiful in southern Portugal. It was designed by master architect André Pilarte, who also worked on the Monastery of Jerónimos in Lisbon. The elaborate carvings feature biblical figures, floral themes, and religious symbols, all with meticulous attention to detail.

Stepping Inside: A Tiled Wonderland.
When you open the large oak doors and go inside, you're welcomed by the warm light of golden altars and the sparkling blue hues of traditional azulejo tiles. These exquisite 17th-century tiles surround the walls, representing the story of the Acts of Mercy, a biblical motif that represents the church's charitable and compassionate mission.

The high altar, decorated with elaborate wood carvings and gilded accents, is a stunning focal point. Looking closely, you'll notice exquisite portrayals of saints, angels, and religious sceneries, all meticulously sculpted by artists from Portugal's golden age of religious art.

A Peaceful Retreat.
Unlike some of Portugal's great churches, Igreja do Misericórdia is peaceful and private. Sitting in one of the pews, you can sense the history that surrounds you—the centuries-old prayers, the wedding and baptism festivities, and the quiet moments of introspection.

Even if you are not religious, this church is worth visiting because of its sheer beauty and artistic skill. Whether you spend five minutes admiring the exterior or an hour inside soaking up the intricacies, it's a place that leaves an impression.

Camera Obscura: Tavira's Most Unique Viewpoint.

At first sight, the Camera Obscura in Tavira appears to be just another medieval tower, but once inside, you'll discover one of Portugal's most amazing optical illusions. The Camera Obscura, housed in the Torre de Tavira, a former water tower converted into a 360-degree periscope, provides a live, moving panoramic image of Tavira in real time using the magic of light and mirrors.

A Journey Across Time and Science

The Camera Obscura is based on an ancient optical theory from Leonardo da Vinci's time. A series of mirrors and lenses cast a moving picture of Tavira onto a white, concave surface in a darkened space. What was the result? A magnificent, real-time "live painting" of the town, replete with people wandering through the streets, boats floating down the river, and birds soaring over Tavira's rooftops.

A Guided Experience Like No Other.
What makes this sight even more unique is the enthusiastic and knowledgeable guides that run the Camera Obscura. They don't simply show you the image; they take you on a narrative journey through Tavira's past. As you watch the town unfold before your eyes, the guide highlights significant landmarks:

- The magnificent Igreja da Misericórdia, with its breathtaking blue-and-white azulejo tiles
- The Roman Bridge, where centuries of footsteps have left an imprint
- The faraway Ria Formosa is a network of rivers leading to golden beaches.
- What is the best part? The view changes based on the time of day, weather, and season, so each visit to the Camera Obscura is unique.

Why You Should Not Miss It
The Camera Obscura provides an innovative and fascinating way to experience Tavira. Not only is it an excellent learning opportunity, but it also offers one of the best panoramic views of the town without the need to climb a hill!

Praça da República is the heart of Tavira.

Tavira's Praça da República is a bright and welcoming location where locals and visitors gather to experience the town's energy. This attractive center square is more than simply a gathering place; it serves as a stage for Tavira's daily life, brimming with history, culture, and a vibrant atmosphere.

A Square Rich in History

For generations, Praça da República has served as Tavira's central hub. In medieval times, it was a thriving marketplace where traders traded fresh fish, fruit, and spices from faraway regions. Later, it became a hub for political and social gatherings, with significant historical events taking place right here.

The statue of Dom Paio Peres Correia, the knight who led Tavira's Christian victory in 1242, is one of the square's most outstanding features. Standing majestically in the center, he serves as a reminder of the town's rich history.

A Place to Slow Down and Take It All In.

Tavira's Praça da República, with its beautiful cafés, restaurants, and pubs, is ideal for leisurely exploration. Order a coffee on one of the outdoor patios, listen to street musicians play soft Fado music, and watch the world go by.

At night, the area becomes a hive of entertainment, with live music, local activities, and even traditional dance performances. If you visit during Tavira's festivals, this is where the festivities truly come to life.

What Makes It So Special?
- A fantastic area to sit and people watch.
- A center for cultural activities and concerts.
- Surrounded by historical structures and gorgeous architecture.

Experience Tavira's atmosphere at Praça da República, whether for a peaceful morning coffee or an evening of music and fun.

Tavira Municipal Museum

For individuals who enjoy learning about a town's history, the Tavira Municipal Museum (Museu Municipal de Tavira) is a must-see. This museum is more than just a single building; it is a collection of historical sites and exhibitions distributed across Tavira, each providing a unique view into the town's intriguing history.

A Museum Like No Other
The museum's exhibitions are spread among numerous main locations, including:

Palácio da Galeria - The main edifice, a splendid 16th-century palace, houses archeological finds, Moorish antiquities, and contemporary art displays.
Casa André Pilarte - A well-preserved medieval mansion that depicts how people lived in Tavira centuries ago.
São Sebastião Church - a former church that now houses religious art and historical items.

Treasures of the Museum
One of the Tavira Municipal Museum's features is its collection of items from the Phoenician, Roman, and Moorish periods. Ancient pottery, money, and tools indicate how this small town once functioned as a vibrant trading hub.

Another remarkable exhibit is the Moorish Tavira area, which displays beautiful Islamic tiles, artistic pottery, and even pieces of old Moorish walls. These remnants depict the tale of Tavira's time under Islamic domination, which influenced much of the town's architecture and culture.

Why It is Worth Visiting

- Great for history buffs - Discover Tavira's history, from prehistoric times to the present.
- Interactive exhibits: Some parts allow visitors to touch and investigate items up close.
- Beautiful sites - The museum is located in spectacular historic buildings, which make it both visually appealing and educational.

For anyone interested in genuinely understanding Tavira's story, the Municipal Museum provides a fascinating and enriching experience.

Final Thoughts: Discovering Tavira's Cultural and Historical Gems

Tavira is a town where the past and contemporary coexist in perfect harmony. The old walls of Tavira Castle, the ageless appeal of the Roman Bridge, the architectural splendor of Igreja da Misericórdia, Camera Obscura, Praça da República, and Municipal Museum, add to the town's enchanting atmosphere telling the story of a town that has stood the test of time.

So take your time. Wander, listen, and absorb the stories woven within Tavira's streets and buildings. Whether you're a history buff, a photography enthusiast, or a visitor looking for real experiences, these must-see sights will make your trip to Tavira absolutely unique.

Hidden Gems in Tavira

Tavira is well-known for its rich history and beautiful beaches, but it also has some pleasant hidden secrets. Beyond the famous tourist attractions, there are areas of town where nature and culture combine in the most beautiful ways. One such location is Pego do Inferno, a hidden and spectacular waterfall nestled in the Algarve's hinterland. Then there's Palácio da Galeria, a wonderful work of art and history that many visitors overlook despite being in the heart of Tavira. These two hidden gems invite you to discover Tavira's lesser-known side, where beauty, history, and nature intersect in almost mysterious ways—as if you've stumbled upon something only a select few may experience.

Pego do Inferno: The Peaceful Paradise.

If you want to enjoy the Algarve's natural splendor in a way that feels like a well-kept secret, visit Pego do Inferno. This spectacular waterfall and its surroundings, located just a short drive from Tavira, provide a calm getaway from the town's hustle and bustle. Getting to Pego do Inferno seems like discovering a secret world—like you're stepping off the beaten route and into a peaceful, even mystical region that few people know about.

As you approach the site, the air becomes cooler, fresher, and scented with pine trees and wildflowers. The climb down to the waterfall is an experience in and of itself, as the path winds through lush foliage, crossing minor streams and rock formations. The sound of rustling foliage and distant bird sounds creates a soothing rhythm as you get closer to the lake. And when you finally arrive, it's like walking into a nature lover's paradise.

The waterfall, tumbling into a small, crystal-clear pool, is quite stunning. It's almost otherworldly—the water cascades down from above, creating a mist that dances in the sunlight. You may feel the chilly shower on your skin as you stand transfixed by the sight. The pool below is appealing, ideal for a refreshing swim if you're feeling daring. The surrounding rocks and rich flora only add to the charm, resulting in a natural amphitheater of peace and beauty. If you're lucky, you may even have the spot to yourself, allowing you to completely appreciate the tranquility of the moment.

While the waterfall is the center attraction, the entire area surrounding Pego do Inferno is lush with vegetation. It's a sanctuary for birders and wildlife lovers. As you walk about, keep a look out for local wildlife, such as a bird of prey soaring overhead or butterflies fluttering amid the blooms. The sense of tranquillity here is unrivaled, making it the ideal destination for those looking to immerse themselves in the natural side of the Algarve away from the throng. Whether you're simply admiring the scenery, taking photos, or sitting peacefully by the lake, Pego do Inferno provides an unforgettable experience in the midst of the region's nature.

Palácio da Galeria: A Step Back in Time.

The Palácio da Galeria, located in the heart of Tavira, is a hidden gem that is sometimes overlooked by the town's more recognized features. This wonderful edifice, a fusion of historical architecture and contemporary art, is a fascinating place to visit, but it remains slightly beneath the radar, which just adds to its appeal.

The palace itself goes back to the 16th century and was initially used as an aristocratic dwelling before becoming the art museum it is today. As you approach the structure, you're met by its beautiful façade—a superb illustration of Tavira's sophisticated architectural style, with elements of Moorish influence combining with Renaissance features from the time. The structure serves as a peaceful reminder of the town's multifaceted history and progress over the years.

Once inside, the Palácio da Galeria reveals its true beauty. The palace's galleries contain collections that highlight Tavira's rich artistic and cultural past. Walking through the halls, you will see an impressive collection of Portuguese paintings, sculptures, and ceramics from various periods. The exhibitions change frequently, so there's always something new to discover. What distinguishes this museum is its ability to provide visitors with an intimate and personal experience of Tavira's cultural depth. There's a sense of calm reverence here, as if the building is conversing with the visitor about the town's illustrious history.

The juxtaposition of old and new in the Palácio da Galeria is striking. The walls are covered with centuries-old artwork, which blends wonderfully with contemporary pieces, creating a dynamic ambiance that is both reflective and modern. Each room is a voyage through time, providing a glimpse of Tavira's artistic development, from medieval craftsmanship to twentieth-century inventiveness.

This place is remarkable for more than simply the artwork. The architecture of the palace tells its own story. As you move from room to room, you'll notice magnificent tilework, elaborate ceiling designs, and an undeniable sense of grandeur derived from centuries of history. The building's inner courtyards are peaceful areas where you can pause, absorb up the tranquil ambiance, and feel transported back in time to a period of aristocratic beauty.

Why Do These Hidden Gems Matter?

Both Pego do Inferno and Palácio da Galeria provide something special for the interested traveler. These spots feel like personal discoveries, where you may connect with Tavira's spirit away from the crowds. They inspire you to take a step back, whether to ponder on the peacefulness of a waterfall or to admire the beauty of a well-preserved historical structure. Visiting these areas is not just about checking off must-see sites, but about experiencing the essence of Tavira in its most authentic form.

São Sebastião Chapel: A Quiet Sanctuary for History and Faith.

The peaceful São Sebastião Chapel is located in the center of Tavira, away from the busy streets. This church, hidden beyond the town's walls and set amid the trees, feels like a personal secret waiting to be revealed. It's an area that encourages peaceful thought, providing a respite from the normal tourist crowds.

The chapel's history is rooted in centuries of religion and tradition. The São Sebastião Chapel, built in the 16th century, was dedicated to St. Sebastian, a Christian martyr and symbol of protection amid plague and epidemic. Tavira, like many other Portuguese towns, experienced multiple epidemics, prompting St. Sebastian to intervene. The chapel was established as a place for people to assemble, worship, and find peace during difficult times.

Even now, its presence serves as a reminder of the town's tenacity and strong faith.

Walking through the chapel's doors, you are immediately immersed in a sense of silent solemnity. Soft, muted light streams through the stained glass windows, creating beautiful reflections on the whitewashed walls. The chapel's baroque altar is stunning, with exquisite carvings and gilded embellishments that ooze history and devotion. The ceiling's wooden beams, decorated with themes and religious symbols, attract your gaze upward, providing a sense of space and height within this little building. São Sebastião Chapel provides a humble and tranquil ambiance for guests to experience moments of stillness.

The chapel is located in a tranquil area of Tavira, surrounded by beautiful trees and quiet streets. This separation from the town's main parts makes it ideal for individuals seeking privacy or a chance to reflect. Whether you're religious or not, there's something incredibly touching about standing in a space so connected to the town's history, a site where generations of Tavirans have come to seek calm and, in many ways, continue to do.

São Sebastião Chapel has a unique blend of spirituality, history, and architecture, making it a must-see attraction. It provides a peaceful and personal setting, ideal for anyone wishing to connect with the town beyond its iconic sights.

Tavira Water Tower: A Glance at the Past

The Tavira Water Tower, another fascinating but underestimated jewel, is just a short walk from Tavira's town, standing tall against the sky. While not as spectacular as Tavira's famed Roman Bridge or stately castle, the Water Tower has its own appeal, providing tourists with insight into the town's history and relationship with water.

The Tavira Water Tower is a 17th-century tower that was initially constructed as part of the town's water distribution system. Tavira, like much of the Algarve, has traditionally relied on wells and water sources to support its inhabitants, particularly during the scorching summer months. The water tower was an important component of the town's water storage and distribution system, ensuring that Tavira residents had access to this vital resource. Today, it serves as a reminder of the town's inventiveness and the role of water in its development.

What distinguishes the Tavira Water Tower is its architecture, which is a magnificent example of the practical beauty that defined much of Portugal's medieval infrastructure. The tower is made of solid stone, and its robust walls convey a feeling of permanence and toughness. Its modest design is unadorned but elegant, with small windows that enable a gentle flow of light into the room. The tower is not open to the public, but the outside alone is enough to pique interest. It's easy to overlook if you're hurrying through Tavira, but if you take the time to enjoy it, you'll notice history inscribed into every stone.

The tower's location, slightly isolated from the town's major streets, provides an ideal setting for a peaceful period of reflection. Whether you stop for a moment to enjoy the tower's basic beauty or merely walk around its base, the Tavira Water Tower is one of those sites that invites you to appreciate the lost intricacies of history. Its silent existence in Tavira reflects the town's numerous layers of life, including how it has adapted, changed, and endured over time.

Why Do These Hidden Gems Matter?

Both São Sebastião Chapel and Tavira Water Tower provide more than just scenic views and historical significance. They are understated reflections of Tavira's deep ties to the past—its challenges, successes, and resilience. These hidden treasures show an often-overlooked aspect of Tavira that is crucial to comprehending the town's identity.

Visiting these locations allows you to get off the beaten tourist road and see Tavira in a more intimate way. São Sebastião Chapel offers a peaceful and spiritual atmosphere, with echoes from centuries past. In contrast, the Tavira Water Tower serves as a reminder of the town's practical resourcefulness and the role of water in defining its growth.

In a town as rich in history as Tavira, it's tempting to get caught up in the larger, more well-known sights. However, the genuine heart of a place can be discovered in quiet corners, forgotten structures, and tranquil areas where history and nature intersect. The São Sebastião Chapel, Pego do Inferno, Palácio da Galeria and Tavira Water Tower are hidden gems that share their history with anyone who are prepared to listen.

Beaches and Islands: Tavira's Coastal Paradise

Tavira is a place where time appears to slow down, where the tides rule the day, and the sea stretches eternally to the horizon. If there's one thing that truly makes this place magical, it's the breathtaking coastline—soft golden sands, crystal-clear waves, and the unspoiled splendor of the Ria Formosa Natural Park.

Here, beaches are more than just places to sunbathe. They are escapes, secret sanctuaries, and natural wonders. Some, such as Ilha de Tavira, are naturally vivacious, brimming with beachgoers and laughing. Others, such as Terra Estreita Beach, feel like well-kept secrets, with the only sound being the calm lapping of the waves. Then there's Ria Formosa, a vast ecosystem of lagoons, sandbanks, and islands waiting to be discovered.

So, kick off your shoes, take a deep breath of salty air, and join us on a journey around Tavira's most stunning beaches and islands.

Ilha de Tavira: A Classic Island Getaway

If you want limitless lengths of smooth sand, warm blue waves, and a relaxed beach atmosphere, Ilha de Tavira is the place to be. This barrier island, located just a short boat trip from Tavira's center, feels like another world—one where summer never stops.

Getting There is Part of the Fun!

Reaching Ilha de Tavira is a little adventure in and of itself. You can take a ferry from Tavira's shoreline, a water taxi, or even a boat excursion that includes a gorgeous ride through Ria Formosa Natural Park and a stop on the island. Whatever route you take, the instant you step off the boat and onto the wooden boardwalks, you will feel as if you have entered a sun-drenched paradise.

Why You Will Love It

Soft, golden sands that spread for kilometers - even during high summer, there is plenty of space.

Beachside restaurants and bars - Enjoy fresh seafood and cold drinks while your toes are in the beach.

The waters are quiet, shallow, and crystal clear, making them ideal for swimming.

Whether you want to soak up the sun, play beach volleyball, or simply walk down the shoreline with the waves tickling your feet, Ilha de Tavira offers the best beach experience.

Praia do Barril: A Beach with a Story.

Praia do Barril is more than just a beach; it's a place where history and nature coexist. Located on another barrier island immediately west of Ilha de Tavira, it is noted for its pristine beauty as well as the frightening yet fascinating "Anchor Cemetery."

A Journey through the Sand Dunes
The journey to Praia do Barril is an experience in itself. Unlike most beaches that need a boat ride, you'll first cross a pedestrian bridge over the Ria Formosa before taking a delightful miniature train or walking along a scenic trail through the dunes. In any case, the minute the wide Atlantic Ocean appears in front of you, you will feel as if you have discovered something unique.

The Anchor Cemetery: A Tribute to Tavira's Fishing Past.

The Cemitério das Âncoras (Anchor Cemetery) is a distinctive feature of Praia do Barril, consisting of hundreds of rusted anchors left behind by tuna fisherman decades ago amid the sand dunes. It's a hauntingly gorgeous scene that reminds Tavira of her strong connection to the sea.

Why is Praia do Barril special?

- A quiet and expansive beach - even in the summer, it never feels crowded.
- A beautiful combination of history and nature: walk among the anchors and learn about historic fishing traditions.
- Ideal for long beach walks - the shoreline goes forever in either direction.

Whether you come to relax, explore, or simply watch the sunset paint the sky, Praia do Barril is a beach that you'll remember long after you leave.

Cabanas Beach: The Locals' Favorite Escape.

Cabanas Beach, which is little less well-known, is where people flock for a calm beach day away from the masses. This quiet stretch of sand is located east of Tavira and is easily accessible by boat from Cabanas hamlet, a lovely fishing village with whitewashed buildings and waterfront cafés.

Why You'll Fall in Love With Cabanas Beach

- A relaxing, unspoiled environment - no large resorts, no crowds, just pure tranquillity.
- Ideal for water sports - Try paddleboarding, kayaking, or windsurfing on the tranquil waters.
- Gorgeous sunsets - Stay until the evening and you'll be treated to one of the most beautiful sunsets in the Algarve.

If you enjoy tranquil, pristine beaches, Cabanas is a hidden gem worth seeing.

Terra Estreita Beach: Tavira's Best Kept Secret

Terra Estreita Beach is the perfect place to feel like you have the entire ocean to yourself. Nestled between Praia do Barril and Ilha de Tavira, this is one of the most quiet and breathtaking locations in the area.

How to Get There.

Unlike the more well-known beaches, Terra Estreita is only accessible by boat from Santa Luzia, a small fishing community noted for its octopus specialties. The brief ride across the lagoon heightens the sense of adventure, making the experience even more special.

Why It is Worth the Extra Effort

- Fewer crowds, more solitude - even in the summer, it's blissfully quiet.
- Perfect for couples and solo travelers seeking a romantic or peaceful vacation.
- Pure, untouched environment - no beach bars or loud music, just the sound of the sea.

Terra Estreita is for those who enjoy the simple pleasures of the sea—the warmth of the sand, the rhythm of the waves, and the never-ending horizon.

Exploring Ria Formosa Natural Park: A Coastal Wonderland.

No trip to Tavira's beaches is complete without seeing the Ria Formosa Natural Park, a breathtaking maze of lagoons, salt marshes, and barrier islands that runs along the Algarve coast.

A Paradise for Nature Lovers.
Ria Formosa is home to remarkable diversity, including:

- Flamingos, spoonbills, and other migrant birds
- Seahorses and marine life in crystal-clear seas.
- Salt pans that sparkle beneath the golden light.

How To Experience It
- Take a boat excursion along the park's rivers.
- Rent a kayak or paddleboard and float across the quiet lagoons.
- Go birdwatching at sunrise for an unforgettable experience.

Whether you prefer to cruise, paddle, or simply sit and enjoy the view, Ria Formosa is a location where nature feels pristine and timeless.

Final Thoughts: Finding Your Ideal Beach Escape

Tavira's shoreline is a dreamscape of golden sands, blue oceans, and hidden treasures waiting to be discovered. Whether you want to soak up the sun on Ilha de Tavira, meander among the anchors at Praia do Barril, or lose yourself in the solitude of Terra Estreita, there's a beach here that feels tailor-made for you.

So let the ocean breeze guide you. Let the waves lull you into a state of complete tranquility. Tavira's beaches invite you to slow down, breathe deeply, and simply be.

Cultural Experiences in Tavira

Tavira is more than just a beautiful town with whitewashed buildings, cobblestone streets, and golden beaches. It's a town where culture pervades every corner, where music fills the air in the evening, where traditions are passionately celebrated, and where art can be found in both historic structures and contemporary galleries.

To truly experience Tavira, you must immerse yourself in its soul—sit in a dimly lit tavern and let the haunting melodies of Fado stir something deep within you; attend a local festival where the streets come alive with music, dance, and fireworks; and wander through art galleries, discovering works that tell the story of the Algarve's past and present.

Let's explore Tavira's cultural heartbeat—the experiences that connect you to its history, people, and everlasting artistic spirit.

Fado Music Nights: A Soulful Sound from Portugal

If one sound characterizes Portugal's soul, it is Fado. This extremely emotional, gloomy song is more than just a performance; it's an expression of love, longing, and saudade, a Portuguese word that translates to a strong sense of nostalgia and yearning.

A Night of Fado in Tavira.
Imagine walking into a tiny, softly lit venue, possibly a modest Fado house hidden away in the old town. The walls are covered in images of previous performers, the smell of red wine and candle wax fills the air, and there is a sense of expectancy.

Then the opening chords of the Portuguese guitar fill the room, a sound so distinct and expressive that it immediately captures your attention. The singer, usually clad in black, begins to sing, their voice conveying the weight of history, love, and longing.

In that moment, time slows. You feel every note and emotion, even if you don't comprehend the words.

Where to Experience Fado in Tavira?

- Fado com História - This compact venue is one of the greatest places to witness true Fado, offering not only live performances but also an insight to the genre's history.
- Local pubs and cultural centers - Look for spontaneous Fado nights in modest taverns and communal venues.

A Fado night in Tavira is more than just a concert; it's an emotional trip that stays with you long after the final song fades.

Local festivals and events: Tavira in celebration.

Tavira may appear tranquil for most of the year, but when festival season arrives, the town changes into a colorful celebration of history, music, and community spirit. These festivals are more than simply for show; they are profoundly ingrained in the town's history, faith, and culture, giving visitors a look into Tavira's spirit.

Festa de São João (Festival of St. John) - June.

Tavira's Festa de São João is a popular celebration that includes music, parades, street entertainment, and traditional food vendors.

During the festivities, expect to witness folks dancing in the streets, eating grilled sardines, and lighting little bonfires.
Fireworks illuminate the night sky, creating a magnificent glow above the Rio Gilão.
The celebration is rooted in ancient pagan customs that commemorate the summer solstice and rejuvenation.

Nossa Senhora da Luz Festival, September

A religious and festive celebration honoring Our Lady of Light, the patron saint of fishermen.

A lovely procession moves through the streets, carrying a statue of the Virgin Mary.
The celebration also features traditional music, folk dancing, and open-air feasts with local delicacies.

Festival de Gastronomia do Mar - A feast for the senses.

If you enjoy food, you should not miss this event! The Seafood Gastronomy Festival, held yearly, is a paradise for visitors looking to sample the freshest seafood meals, local wines, and traditional Algarvean specialties.

Restaurants in Tavira participate, with special menus featuring octopus, clams, and grilled fish.

Cooking demos and live music enhance the joyful ambiance.

Tavira always has something to celebrate, regardless of when you arrive. What is the best way to experience these festivals? Join the people, dance in the streets, and be caught up in the excitement of it all.

Art Galleries and Exhibitions: Tavira's Creative Spirit

Tavira has long been a shelter for artists, writers, and creative souls lured by its distinct light, history, and atmosphere. Art can be found everywhere here—not just in galleries, but also in the streets, old buildings converted as exhibition spaces, and even modest artisan workshops where craftspeople keep traditional techniques alive.

Palácio da Galeria: Where History and Art Meet.

The Palácio da Galeria, located in a stunning 16th-century palace, is Tavira's most important art location.

It features recurring contemporary art exhibitions by Portuguese and international artists.

Archaeological ruins dating back to the Phoenicians can be found beneath the palace, serving as a reminder of Tavira's close relationship with art and history.

The displays frequently explore topics of Algarvean identity, history, and nature, making it a must-see for those seeking to grasp the region's artistic character.

Tavira d'Artes: A Gathering of Local Talent

For a more grassroots artistic experience, stop into Tavira d'Artes, an artists' group and gallery space.

You can view (and purchase) works by local painters, sculptors, and photographers.

It's an excellent spot to find handcrafted ceramics, fabrics, and jewelry—ideal keepsakes with a personal touch.

Street Art and Public Installations

Tavira's art scene isn't limited to galleries; when you walk throughout town, you'll notice:

- Azulejo tile murals convey stories about the town's past.
- Small artistic interventions in hidden spaces, ranging from painted doors to mosaic benches.
- Temporary outdoor exhibitions, usually set up in public places.

If you have an artistic soul, Tavira will nourish your creativity at every turn.

Final thoughts: Tavira's Cultural Heartbeat

To properly understand Tavira, you must experience its culture—the melancholy yet beautiful songs of Fado, the memorable intensity of its festivals, and the art that recounts its story. It's a town that encourages you to listen, rejoice, and be inspired.

So visit a Fado house, join the villagers in a festival procession, or get lost in a gallery.

Tavira's cultural experiences are more than just sights to see; they are moments to feel, enjoy, and remember.

Gastronomy in Tavira

Tavira, with its sun-kissed beaches, lush landscapes, and rich cultural legacy, provides not just magnificent beauty but also a culinary experience as colorful and diverse as the town itself. Tavira's flavors are a sensory pleasure, drawing on centuries of tradition and local ingredients to create a gastronomic experience that will tingle your taste buds and fill your heart.

The Algarve's seaside riches, including fresh seafood, tender meats, and fragrant herbs, all play an important role in the town's culinary scene. Whether you're strolling through Tavira's picturesque streets, having a lengthy lunch on a sun-dappled terrace, or exploring the local markets, the region's delicacies are always within reach. Let's go on a culinary tour around Tavira, where every meal is a celebration and each dish tells a tale.

Traditional Dishes to Try: A Taste of Tavira

To properly appreciate Tavira, you must try its traditional cuisine, each one paying homage to the town's rich heritage and coastal riches.

1. **Cataplana de Mariscos, or Seafood Cataplana**

This is the center of Algarve cuisine: a fragrant, acidic seafood stew that serves as both a meal and a ritual. This dish, served in a copper pot (a "cataplana"), combines an assortment of fresh seafood—clams, shrimp, mussels, and tender fish—in a broth laced with garlic, tomatoes, onions, white wine, and herbs. When you lift the cover, fragrant steam rises, enticing your senses, and the delicate sweetness of the shellfish combines with the thick, aromatic broth.

2. **Arroz de Marisco (seafood rice).**

Arroz de Marisco, a near cousin of cataplana, is a rice-centric dish. Cooked slowly in a rich, seafood-infused broth, the rice absorbs all of the flavors, resulting in a creamy, comforting texture. This meal, packed with the freshest clams, prawns, and cuttlefish, is a true celebration of Tavira's coastal wealth.

3. **Polvo à Lagareiro (Octopus with Olive Oil)**

In Tavira, octopus is considered an art form. Polvo à Lagareiro is a delectable dish in which octopus is grilled to perfection and then drizzled with premium olive oil, garlic, and fresh herbs. The delicate, slightly smokey octopus is accented with roasted potatoes, resulting in a dish that is both luxurious and simple, but full of flavor.

4. Feijão Frade (black-eyed peas)

Tavira's rustic side may be tasted in Feijão Frade, a cozy stew with black-eyed peas, succulent pork, and simmering vegetables. This meal is commonly served as a robust addition to seafood or grilled meats, providing a pleasing earthiness that complements the lighter flavors of the coast.

5. Doce Fino (The Algarve's Sweet Delight)

For dessert, try Doce Fino, a sweet, comforting almond-based delight that is a true Algarve treasure. The thin pastry is filled with sweet, velvety almond cream and often sprinkled with powdered sugar, resulting in a bite-sized delight that is both rich and savory.

Top Restaurants in Tavira: Culinary Havens

Tavira has a range of restaurants that provide both traditional Portuguese cuisine and inventive meals that highlight the best of local products. Tavira's restaurants cater to all tastes and occasions, from a lovely seafood restaurant by the river to a sophisticated eatery with breathtaking views.

1. Restaurante Brasa do Rio

Restaurante Brisa do Rio, located on the riverfront, offers breathtaking views of the Rio Gilão and surrounding countryside. This restaurant, famous for its grilled fish and seafood cataplanas, offers the traditional Tavira experience. The environment is calm, with wooden tables beneath the shade of huge trees, and the food is as fresh as it gets. The flavors are fresh, strong, and rich, highlighting the best of the Algarve's seafood.

2. O Castelo

O Castelo, located near Tavira Castle, serves traditional Portuguese cuisine with a modern twist. It's an ideal location for a romantic dinner with great views of the town. Favorites on the menu include grilled sardines, seafood rice, and sumptuous local wines. The environment is cozy and warm, making it popular with both residents and tourists.

3. Casa do Rio

If you want something a little more modern and trendy, Casa do Rio serves unique food with a focus on sustainability and locally sourced products. This sleek, contemporary restaurant is located near the lake and serves seasonal veggies and fresh fish. Each dish's presentation is as appealing as its flavors, making this a destination for both foodies and aesthetics enthusiasts.

4. A Taska

A Taska provides a more relaxed, authentic experience with a selection of tapas-style plates and a pleasant ambiance that feels like home. This lovely restaurant serves local delights such as grilled chorizo, octopus salad, and a variety of cheeses. It is a gathering place for locals to have a glass of wine while savoring Tavira's traditional flavors.

Local Markets and Food Tours: A Taste of Tavira's Heart

To really grasp Tavira's food culture, a trip to one of the local markets or a guided food tour is required. You'll not only see where people buy their vegetables, but you'll also get to sample the region's authentic flavors.

1. Tavira Municipal Market

A visit to the Tavira Municipal Market is like entering the heart of the town's culinary culture. The market, situated in a stunning traditional structure, is a sensory assault of color, music, and fragrance. Fresh seafood, luscious fruits, locally grown veggies, and artisan cheeses are beautifully exhibited by friendly local sellers.

The market is also a terrific place to try some local cured meats, olives, and fresh bread, which are ideal for a riverside picnic. If you go in the morning, don't pass up the opportunity to enjoy a pastel de nata—a warm, custardy Portuguese pastry that will take you to a realm of luxury.

2. Tavira Food Tours

A food tour is the ideal way to explore Tavira's hidden gastronomic wonders. These tours, led by dedicated local guides, take you through Tavira's meandering alleyways, stopping at local cafés, marketplaces, and family-run restaurants that you may not have discovered otherwise. You will sample regional specialties, drink local wines, and learn about the history and culture of each dish.

Last Thoughts: A Culinary Escape in Tavira

Tavira's gastronomy celebrates the town's rich history, coastal richness, and agricultural heritage. From the delicate, fragrant cataplanas to the handcrafted pastries, each bite tells a tale. So, whether you're enjoying a leisurely dinner in a riverfront restaurant, browsing the bustling markets, or engaging in a food tour, Tavira welcomes you to feast like a local and cherish each delectable moment.

Outdoor Activities in Tavira

Tavira, set amid the Algarve's undulating hills and sun-kissed beaches, is an outdoor enthusiast's heaven. The town's unique blend of coastline beauty, rough landscapes, and calm canals make it an ideal destination for adventurers and nature lovers. Whether you're a seasoned hiker, a bird-watching enthusiast, a water sports fanatic, or a golf aficionado, Tavira has a plethora of outdoor activities to encourage you to explore every inch of this breathtaking region. Are you ready to unleash your adventurous spirit? Let's explore the exciting world of outdoor activities in Tavira!

Hiking and Nature Trails: Discover the Algarve's Hidden Beauty.

Tavira is a hiker's paradise, where nature's beauty reveals at every turn, with breathtaking routes and hidden jewels waiting to be discovered. There are trails for every level of adventurer, from moderate hills in the countryside to stunning cliffs along the shore. Lace up your boots and hit the trails to see Tavira from a completely new perspective.

1. Via Algarviana

For those seeking a hard adventure, the Via Algarviana is an iconic long-distance trail that runs from the Spanish border to Cape St. Vincent, providing breathtaking vistas of the Algarve landscape. This route leads through Tavira's verdant hills and woodlands, where you'll see olive gardens, cork oak forests, and wildflowers. The natural splendor of this walk, with its wide-open skies and serene seclusion, will leave you feeling invigorated and inspired.

2. Rota Vicentina

Another excellent hiking option is the Rota Vicentina, a network of trails that runs along the Algarve's spectacular coastline. Consider the Fisherman's Trail, which follows the cliffs and provides stunning views of the turquoise sea and craggy shoreline. This hike will immerse you in the raw beauty of Tavira's shore, with the sound of waves breaking against the rocks providing a soundtrack to your journey.

3. Ilha de Tavira Trails

For a more leisurely coastline experience, visit the picturesque Ilha de Tavira, a tranquil island accessible by ferry. This natural reserve has a variety of trails across sand dunes, salt marshes, and pine forests. The island's flat topography and picturesque views of the sea make it an ideal location for trekking and birdwatching.

With so many beautiful routes to select from, Tavira provides a hiking trip for both novice and experienced explorers alike.

Bird Watching in Ria Formosa: A Bird Lover's Paradise

Tavira's proximity to the Ria Formosa Natural Park makes it a birdwatching hotspot. This 18,000-hectare coastal lagoon is one of Europe's most important bird habitats, supporting over 200 species of birds such as flamingos, herons, and spoonbills. Whether you're a beginner or an experienced birdwatcher, the Ria Formosa provides a unique opportunity to witness these amazing creatures in their native habitat.

1. **Bird watching in Cacela Velha**
The Cacela Velha region, located just east of Tavira, is ideal for bird watching. Its salt flats, dunes, and marshes make an excellent

backdrop for observing a variety of species, especially during their spring and autumn migrations. With a little patience, you can spot pale-bellied Brent geese and the secretive great white egret.

2. Guided Bird Watching Tours

If you wish to go deeper into the realm of birdwatching, take a guided trip of the Ria Formosa. Local specialists will not only assist you identify the numerous species, but they will also provide intriguing insights into the park's delicate ecosystem. These tours frequently take you along quiet roads and hidden areas where you can spot uncommon animals with the help of an experienced guide.

3. Ria Formosa Observation Posts

Tavira has various observation sites placed throughout the Ria Formosa that will enhance your birdwatching experience. These intentionally located places provide panoramic views of the wetlands, allowing you to see birds without harming their natural habitat. With the correct binoculars, you may immerse yourself in a world of colorful feathery creatures.

Boat Tours and Water Sports: Set Sail on Tavira's waters.

Tavira's coastal position and serene waters of the Rio Gilão and Ria Formosa make it a great destination for water enthusiasts. Tavira's waterways provide limitless chances for fun and adventure, whether you enjoy relaxing boat trips, exhilarating water sports, or a combination of the two.

1. Boat Tours of Ria Formosa

There is something special about visiting Tavira's coastline and quiet lagoon by boat. Ria Formosa has a distinctive environment of islands, sandbars, and marshes that are best explored by boat. Whether you choose a classic fishing boat or a more modern sailboat, you will glide through tranquil waters while surrounded by nature's beauty. Some tours even include stops at secret beaches where you may cool down or relax on the sand.

2. Kayaking and Stand Up Paddleboarding

For a more hands-on experience, try kayaking or stand-up paddleboarding in Tavira's quiet, sheltered waters. Paddle through the tranquil inlets of the Ria Formosa, where the smooth ebb and flow of the tide creates a peaceful atmosphere. Whether you're exploring the coastline, seeing the salt flats, or navigating the canals of Ilha de Tavira, these activities provide the ideal balance of exercise and exploration.

3. **Windsurfing and kitesurfing**

Tavira's coastal winds make it a great location for windsurfing and kiteboarding. The Atlantic Ocean and Ria Formosa offer both calm and demanding conditions, so there's plenty of room for both beginners and expert surfers. Several local schools provide lessons for individuals interested in getting into the sport, and rental equipment is available for those who are ready to tackle the waves.

Golf Courses: Improve Your Swing in Tavira's Beautiful Landscape

Tavira is also home to some of Portugal's most gorgeous and demanding golf courses, providing the ideal balance of sport, relaxation, and breathtaking vistas. Tavira's golf courses provide a wonderful experience, whether you're an avid golfer or a beginner seeking for a relaxing round.

1. **Benamor Golf**

Benamor Golf, located in the hills close outside Tavira, is one of the region's most well-known courses. This 18-hole course, set against a backdrop of rolling hills and spectacular sea views, is the ideal combination of challenging holes and breathtaking surroundings. Benamor Golf is popular among golfers of all skill levels because to its well-maintained fairways.

2. **Monte Rei Golf and Country Club**

Monte Rei Golf & Country Club, located just a short drive from Tavira, provides an outstanding golfing experience. This five-star resort is home to one of Portugal's top golf courses, created by Jack Nicklaus. Monte Rei is a golfer's paradise, with beautiful fairways, tough greens, and first-rate service.

Final Thoughts: Adventure awaits in Tavira

Tavira is a true outdoor paradise, with several activities that allow you to connect with nature, push yourself, and make great memories. Tavira has something for everyone, from hiking steep trails to boating along the coast, finding endangered birds to refining your golf swing. So, pack your kit, step outside, and let Tavira's scenery feed your adventurous spirit. Adventure is waiting!

Day Trips from Tavira

While Tavira is a treasure trove of beauty and culture, its location in the center of the Algarve provides an ideal starting point for interesting day trips to other cities, natural wonders, and even a neighboring nation. Whether you want to explore more of the magnificent Algarve coastline, meander through quaint old villages, or travel into Spain for a change of pace, Tavira makes it easy to discover the neighboring beauties. Ready to learn more? Here are a few fantastic day trips from Tavira that promise new experiences, hidden gems, and lasting memories.

Visit to Cacela Velha: A Glimpse of Timeless Charm

Cacela Velha, just a 15-minute drive from Tavira, is reminiscent of a postcard. This small hilltop village combines spectacular sea views, whitewashed buildings, and historic ruins, all in a peaceful ambiance. It's one of those spots that instantly transports you back in time while providing breathtaking vistas that will have you wanting to stay forever.

What To Do In Cacela Velha

Cacela Velha's charm will grab you as you walk its cobblestone alleys. The Cacela Velha Fortress proudly overlooks the enormous Atlantic Ocean, with panoramic views of the Ria Formosa Natural Park and the surrounding shoreline. Don't miss the little plaza, which is dotted with local cafes where you can relax and sip a coffee while taking in the charming charm.

For a memorable experience, go to Cacela Velha Beach, one of the Algarve's most beautiful expanses of sand. This beach, which is easily accessible by foot from the village, is frequently calmer than other local beaches, providing a secluded respite with crystal-clear seas and a tranquil atmosphere. Cacela Velha is a must-see for those seeking an idyllic retreat with history and visual beauty.

Explore Faro: The Heart of the Algarve.

Faro, a 30-minute drive from Tavira, is sometimes neglected by tourists, despite being a hidden gem rich in history, culture, and charm. Faro, the capital of the Algarve area, is a dynamic combination of classic Portuguese architecture, bustling streets, and fascinating historical monuments that will make your day trip unforgettable.

What to do in Faro

Begin your tour at Faro's Old Town (Cidade Velha), where you may wander through narrow, cobblestoned alleyways dotted with whitewashed buildings ornamented with colorful tiles. The Arco da Vila is a stunning archway that marks the entrance to the Old Town, taking you through a maze of antique charm. One of the highlights of this area is the Carmo Church (Igreja do Carmo), which is famous for its Chapel of Bones, where the walls are adorned with the skulls and bones of former monks—a fascinating yet terrifying sight!

For a calm afternoon, go to the Faro Marina and take a walk along the lake, surrounded by boats and the distant horizon. The neighboring Ria Formosa Natural Park provides boat tours through the wetlands, allowing you to observe native species and birds in their natural habitat. Faro offers a rich and diverse experience for each traveler, whether you're touring the Old Town, learning about the city's history, or simply relaxing by the sea.

Trip to Olhão: A Fisherman's Delight

Olhão, a fishing town about 30 minutes from Tavira, is a less-touristy and authentic place that offers a look into traditional Algarve life. The town is noted for its distinctive Moorish-style architecture, colorful fish markets, and closeness to the Ria Formosa Natural Park, making it an excellent day excursion for anyone interested in experiencing local culture.

What to do in Olhão?

Begin your journey in the Olhão Fish Market, a must-see for fresh seafood and a sense of local culture. The market is a sensory experience, with the aroma of fresh fish, the buzz of discussion, and the vibrant colors of the day's catch all around. It's an excellent site to see the traditional aspect of the Algarve's fishing culture.

Take a trip along the Olhão waterfront, where you may find lovely cafes and shops selling local products. For a tranquil break, take a ferry to the surrounding islands of Ilha da Culatra and Ilha do Farol, which are only a short boat ride away and offer calm beaches, crystal-clear waters, and breathtaking views of the Ria Formosa lagoon. Take a leisurely walk around the Olhão Historic Center, where tiny lanes and whitewashed cottages add to the town's beauty. Olhão is a calm destination with thriving local life and a slower pace, ideal for a relaxing day vacation.

Journey to Seville, Spain: A Taste of Andalusia.

If you're ready to travel borders and discover more of what Southern Europe has to offer, why not visit Spain? Seville, roughly a two-hour drive or bus ride from Tavira, is an amazing location rich in Spanish history, vibrant culture, and iconic architecture.

What to Do in Seville?

Seville is a city that dazzles with Moorish and Gothic architecture, and one of the first places to see is the Alcázar of Seville, a gorgeous palace complex with elaborate tilework, lush gardens, and breathtaking courtyards. This UNESCO World Heritage Site will transport you through the history of Spain's governing dynasties, and its grounds are ideal for a relaxing stroll.

Next, visit Seville Cathedral, the world's biggest Gothic cathedral, and climb the Giralda Tower for spectacular views of the city. If you have time, explore the Santa Cruz area, which is a maze of little streets and gorgeous squares, or unwind with a glass of sangria in a plaza while taking in the bustling scene. If you enjoy flamenco, attend a performance at one of the local tablaos to experience the soul of Andalusia via song and dance.

Seville's rich culture, fascinating history, and energetic environment make for an unforgettable day excursion that transports you to a world of beauty, passion, and color.

Final Thoughts: Day Trips That Inspire the Spirit of Exploration.

The beauty of Tavira is that, while it is a tranquil, attractive town in its own right, it also serves as an excellent starting point for exploring the surrounding attractions. Discover unique day adventures in Cacela Velha, Faro, Olhão, and Seville, each with their own charm. So grab your hat, put on your walking shoes, and embark on a tour to discover the best of the Algarve and beyond. Adventure is right around the corner!

Practical Information

Traveling to a new location can be thrilling, but it's always useful to have some practical knowledge on hand to make your stay more comfortable and pleasurable. Tavira, with its inviting environment and breathtaking scenery, provides all of the amenities you require for a pleasant visit. In this section, we'll go over some important topics concerning currency and banking, language and communication, safety precautions, and health and medical facilities, so you may feel confident and prepared for your trip.

Currency & Banking

Tavira, like the rest of Portugal, has the Euro as its official currency. When visiting Tavira, you should be informed of how to handle money during your stay.

Cash and Cards

ATMs are readily available in Tavira and are normally open 24 hours a day, seven days a week. They can be found near the town center, shopping areas, and larger supermarkets. Most restaurants, shops, and lodgings accept credit and debit cards, particularly in tourist-friendly locations. However, it is always a good idea to have extra cash on hand for minor purchases, such as those from local markets or cafes that do not accept credit cards.

If you wish to exchange currencies, currency exchange offices are available in Tavira's main commercial areas. Be aware that exchange rates and any additional fees may vary.

Bank Hours
Most banks in Tavira are open from 9:00 a.m. to 3:00 p.m., Monday through Friday. Many of them also have self-service devices available outside of banking hours for cash withdrawals and other transactions. If you have more specialized banking needs, be sure to check the bank's operation hours.

Language & Communication

The official language of Tavira and the rest of Portugal is Portuguese, however many individuals, particularly in tourist areas, speak English. However, knowing a few simple phrases in Portuguese is usually a good idea because it demonstrates respect for the local culture and can enhance your experience. Here are some helpful sentences to get you started:

Olá (Hello)
Bom dia (Good morning)
Boa tarde (Good afternoon)
Boa noite (Good evening)
Por favor (Please)
Obrigado/Obrigada   (Thank   you   –
male/female)
Quanto custa? (How much does it cost?)
Onde fica...? (Where is...?)

Communication and Internet

Most cafes, restaurants, and hotels in Tavira provide free Wi-Fi to their clients, so you'll have no trouble staying connected. If you plan to stay in Tavira for a lengthy amount of time, you might consider acquiring a local SIM card with data. Mobile network companies such as NOS, MEO, and Vodafone provide prepaid SIM cards with a variety of data bundles. These are easily purchased at mobile phone outlets or major supermarkets.

Emergency Numbers

In case of emergency, here are some vital numbers to remember:

Emergency Services (Police, Fire, Medical): 112.

Police: 112 or 218 432 122.

Ambulance: 112.

Even if you don't think you'll need it, it's a good idea to keep the emergency number ready.

Safety Tips

Portugal, particularly Tavira, is well-known as a safe travel destination. Violent crime is uncommon, but like with any vacation, there are general safety precautions to take to guarantee a worry-free trip.

Pickpocketing

While Tavira is a reasonably safe town, pickpocketing can occur, particularly in popular tourist areas or on public transit. Keep your items close to you and use caution in crowded areas such as markets or tourist attractions. Keep your valuables protected with a money belt or a crossbody bag.

Road Safety

If you're thinking of renting a car in Tavira, keep in mind that traffic can be congested in the main towns. Always follow speed restrictions and traffic signs. When strolling about town, use pedestrian crossings and use caution around roundabouts or major crossroads. Parking is normally straightforward in Tavira, however be aware of any parking restrictions to avoid fines.

Health & Weather
Tavira experiences mild weather for much of the year, particularly in the summer months when temperatures can exceed 30°C (86°F). Stay hydrated and wear sunscreen to protect yourself from the sun's harmful rays. Wearing a hat or seeking shade during the warmest hours of the day is also a smart option.

Health and Medical Services

Tavira offers a wide range of healthcare services to both inhabitants and visitors. Portugal's healthcare system is well-regarded, and Tavira is no exception when it comes to providing medical care when needed.

Pharmacies
Tavira has many of pharmacies (or farmácias), which are typically open from 9:00 AM to 1:00 PM and 3:00 PM to 7:00 PM, Monday through Saturday. Some may be open for fewer hours on Sunday. Pharmacies are able to provide

Traveler Tips

Traveling to a new destination, such as Tavira, is more than just sightseeing; it is also about interacting with the local culture, honoring customs, and making a positive impact on the society. To help you make the most of your stay while remaining careful of your surroundings, here are some helpful traveler advice on etiquette and local customs, sustainable tourism practices, and useful applications and websites. These recommendations will not only improve your trip, but will also make you feel like a conscientious and responsible traveler.

Etiquette and Local Customs

One of the finest ways to genuinely experience Tavira is to follow local customs and respect the people and culture. Portugal, in general, is known for being kind, inviting, and proud of its heritage. Here are a few easy politeness recommendations to remember while in Tavira.

Greetings and politeness
When meeting someone in Tavira, a cheerful "Olá" (hello) or "Bom dia" (good morning) might go a long way. Portuguese people are

known for their politeness and formality, especially when meeting new people. A handshake is a usual greeting, however if you're meeting a friend or someone you know well, a gentle kiss on both cheeks is also a nice gesture (though this may vary by location). Even if you don't speak Portuguese fluently, using a few fundamental phrases is usually appreciated. A simple "Obrigado" (thank you) or "Por favor" (please) will demonstrate respect for the local culture and result in a warm grin.

Dinner Etiquette
Tavira, like the rest of Portugal, values its food, therefore mealtime is an important ritual. When you are invited to someone's home for a meal, it is usual to offer a modest gift as a sign of thanks. A bottle of wine, some local delicacies, or an arrangement of flowers are always a good choice. Wait for the host to say "Bom apetite" before you start eating.

When dining out, especially at a traditional Portuguese restaurant, it is common to be offered numerous dishes, beginning with bread and olives (which are frequently complimentary). Don't feel forced to eat everything, but definitely try some of the local delicacies, such as bacalhau (salted codfish) or caldo verde (green soup). Tipping is optional but appreciated at the end of your dinner, often ranging from 5 to 10%.

Public Behavior
Portugal has a laid-back attitude, yet it is crucial to maintain a feeling of modesty and respect, especially in more rural or traditional settings. Be aware of volume when conversing in public places such as cafes or public transportation. The Portuguese prefer a quieter, more meditative setting, thus loud talks or exuberant behavior may draw unwanted attention. Remember that public demonstrations of affection are typically kept modest. While the attitude in Tavira is amicable and laid-back, it is critical to maintain the courteous demeanor that one would expect in any culturally significant city.

Sustainable Tourism Practices

As travelers, we all have a responsibility to conserve the environment and help the local communities. Tavira, with its gorgeous beaches and natural parks, is particularly vulnerable to environmental challenges, therefore travel wisely and sustainably. Here are some practical advice for being an environmentally friendly traveler in Tavira.

Respect nature and wildlife.

Tavira serves as a gateway to the Ria Formosa Natural Park, a one-of-a-kind coastal lagoon teeming with wildlife and vegetation. As a visitor, it is critical to respect this vulnerable habitat. Follow indicated pathways and avoid upsetting wildlife. If you plan to visit the islands or go birdwatching in the park, stay away from wildlife and avoid feeding them.

When visiting the beach, avoid leaving trash behind—this is a general rule, but it is especially vital in locations like Tavira, where the beaches are a major lure. Bring reusable water bottles, keep your litter in your bag until you find a good bin, and try to use as little single-use plastics as possible. If you enjoy snorkeling or kayaking, be cautious of the sensitive marine life beneath the surface. These tiny efforts, taken together, can have a significant impact.

Support Local Businesses.

Supporting local businesses is one of the finest ways to have a good impact in Tavira. Tavira thrives on handcrafted items, small restaurants, and family-run businesses. You may help ensure the community's long-term prosperity by shopping at local markets, dining at smaller restaurants, and staying in locally-owned hotels. Choose eco-friendly hotels that support sustainable practices, such as energy-saving systems and waste reduction initiatives.

Water Conservation

Water conservation is becoming increasingly important, particularly in places with long, dry summers. Tavira, like all of the Algarve, relies heavily on water resources, thus try to utilize them as little as possible. Simple changes, such as taking shorter showers and turning off faucets while not in use, can make a difference. If you're staying somewhere with a swimming pool, make sure you follow any poolside guidelines about usage to help preserve water.

Useful Apps and Resources

Traveling today has become lot easier thanks to technological advancements. Here are some apps and tools that you will find useful during your stay in Tavira:

Google Maps

Google Maps is a useful tool for navigating Tavira's streets and orienting yourself. It will assist you in locating restaurants, activities, and transportation alternatives, as well as providing real-time walking directions if you are traveling by foot.

Tavira Official Tourism App.

Many cities, like Tavira, have specific tourism apps. The Tavira Official Tourism App is an excellent source for local events, sightseeing information, and thorough maps of the area. It is a useful resource for newbies and keeps you up to date on what to do throughout your visit.

TripAdvisor

TripAdvisor is a reliable app for finding restaurants and accommodations. Travelers share their experiences and reviews, allowing you to discover the greatest sites in Tavira based on what other guests have enjoyed. You can also read recommendations from other travelers on what to do, hidden treasures, and places to see.

Sustainable Travel Apps

If you're interested in sustainability, there are several applications dedicated to eco-friendly travel. Green Key is a global designation for environmentally responsible tourism facilities, and HappyCow can help you identify vegan and vegetarian eateries, many of which use sustainable food sourcing.

Final Thoughts

Traveling to Tavira is a unique experience, and with a few basic suggestions on etiquette, sustainability, and the finest applications, you can make your trip both pleasurable and responsible. Remember that being a courteous traveler entails much more than simply observing the rules; it also entails caring for the people, culture, and environment that contribute to Tavira's beauty. Enjoy every minute and travel with care.

Conclusion

Tavira is more than simply a lovely town; it's an invitation to slow down, embrace simplicity, and immerse yourself in the splendor of nature, history, and culture. Tavira's sun-dappled alleys and golden beaches, as well as its rich traditions and hidden gems, create a location that feels both timeless and refreshingly modern. Whether you've gone through the medieval castle walls, strolled down the river with the Roman Bridge as a background, or simply sat back and absorbed the flavors of the local cuisine, Tavira has a way of leaving an impression on you.

Let's go over the main highlights of Tavira and conclude with some final advice to make your holiday here genuinely unforgettable.

Summary of Tavira's Highlights

Tavira, often regarded as one of the most beautiful cities in the Algarve, provides a delightful variety of activities to satisfy every traveler's preferences. Its allure stems from its seamless blend of old history and modern amenities, allowing you to explore at your own speed.

Historical Treasures

Tavira's Castle is an excellent site to begin your adventure through time. With panoramic views of the town, there are opportunities for bird viewing. Tavira's beaches, including Ilha de Tavira and Praia do Barril, are some of the best in the Algarve, ideal for relaxation or aquatic activities. These beaches offer a peaceful escape from the rush and bustle of daily life, allowing you to reconnect with nature.

A Must-see for Local Culture

Tavira is more than just exploring sights; it is also about connecting with the local culture. Wander through the town's lovely streets to find vibrant local markets selling fresh food and regional specialties. The town's Fado nights are a deep dive into Portuguese music, filled with emotion and storytelling. Tavira also organizes local festivals every year, celebrating everything from gastronomy to folklore. These celebrations allow you to experience the heart and soul of Tavira's traditions firsthand.

Final Tips for a Memorable Vacation

As your trip to Tavira approaches, here are some final advice to ensure that your time here is filled with unforgettable experiences and a sense of accomplishment.

Embrace the slow pace.
Tavira is best enjoyed at its relaxed pace. Do not speed through the attractions; instead, cherish each minute. Wander the cobblestone streets, relax at a cafe and watch the world go by, or enjoy a long walk along the river. Tavira's allure lies not only in its scenery, but also in the way it encourages you to slow down and live in the moment. Trust that the most memorable times are frequently spent quietly enjoying the landscape, breathing in the sea air, and simply being there.

Interact with locals.
Tavira's beauty stems not just from its landscapes, but also from its people. Engage with the locals, whether by talking to a market vendor or asking your waiter about the best local delicacies. The warmth and kindness of Tavira's citizens will enhance your experience and give you a stronger connection to the town. Be receptive to their experiences,

recommendations, and ideas; they are the key to discovering Tavira beyond its tourist attractions.

Respect the Environment.
As you explore Tavira, keep sustainability in mind. Consider your environmental effect when visiting the Ria Formosa Natural Park or relaxing on one of the gorgeous beaches. Simple activities like as utilizing reusable water bottles, avoiding plastic trash, and respecting wildlife can help preserve Tavira's beauty for future generations. Sustainable travel is more than a trend; it is a philosophy that may help conserve the places we love to visit.

Plan for Some Spontaneity
While an itinerary is useful, make room for improvisation during your vacation. Tavira has the ability to disclose hidden jewels when you least expect it. Whether it's finding a quiet area on the beach or stumbling into a local artisan's shop, some of the best travel experiences happen unexpectedly. Allow yourself to get lost in Tavira's small streets, and you could find something extraordinary.

Final Reflection

Tavira is a place that provides a sense of calm, discovery, and community. Tavira has the ability to leave a lasting impression, whether you are fascinated by its historical allure, enthralled by its natural beauty, or charmed by the authenticity of its culture. By enjoying the town's slower pace, mingling with its residents, and appreciating its environment, you'll make memories that will last long after you return home.

So, as you consider your next actions, keep in mind that Tavira is more than just a location on a map. It's an invitation to immerse yourself in a world of stories, flavors, sounds, and sights all waiting for you to discover. Take a deep breath, enjoy each moment, and let Tavira work its magic on you.

Printed in Dunstable, United Kingdom

67570237R00060